All sport is …..

Impressum:

Bibliografische Information der Deutschen
Nationalbibliothek: Die Deutsche
Nationalbibliothek verzeichnet diese Publikation
in der Deutschen Nationalbibliografie;
detaillierte bibliografische Daten sind im
Internet über www.dnb.de abrufbar.

© 2020 Peter Oberfrank – Hunziker
Herstellung und Verlag
BoD – Books on Demand, Norderstedt

ISBN 9783746061603

All sport is ….. being in nature, walking, going, running, doing yoga, icehockey, football, tennis, softballtennis, swimming, skiing, sledging, basketball, volleyball, american football, leichtathletik, gymnastic, dancing, handball, surfing, waveboarding, skateboarding, hiking, baseballing …..

My Harvord university diploma is
sporti for me Peter Oberfrank –
Hunziker

good thinking and doing:
universitying
naturingi
celebratingo

Happy and joyful celebrating the NHL (= National Hockey League) as general sports league

Ever celebrating the NHL Stanley Cup trophies and stoni …. with playing the funny icehockeysystem and sportssystem zaroni and vone ….

PETER

creativity and playing